The Truth about
CASTLES

The Truth about CASTLES

Gillian Clements

Carolrhoda Books, Inc./Minneapolis

This edition first published 1990 by Carolrhoda Books, Inc.
Original edition published 1988 by Macmillan Children's
Books, a division of Macmillan Publishers Limited, London.
Original edition copyright © 1988 by Gillian Clements
Additional text copyright © 1990 by Carolrhoda Books, Inc.

Clements, Gillian.
    The truth about castles / Gillian Clements.
        p.   cm.
    Summary: Text and detailed humorous illustrations present an
overview of castles: who made them; when, how, why, and where they
were built; what they were for; and what it was like to live in a
castle.
    ISBN 0-87614-401-6 (lib. bdg.)
    1. Castles—Juvenile literature. 2. Civilization, Medieval—
Juvenile literature. [1. Castles. 2. Civilization, Medieval.]
I. Title.
GT3550.C44   1990   89-22231
940.1—dc20   CIP
                                                                  AC

Manufactured in the United States of America

1 2 3 4 5 6 7 8 9 10 99 98 97 96 95 94 93 92 91 90

CONTENTS

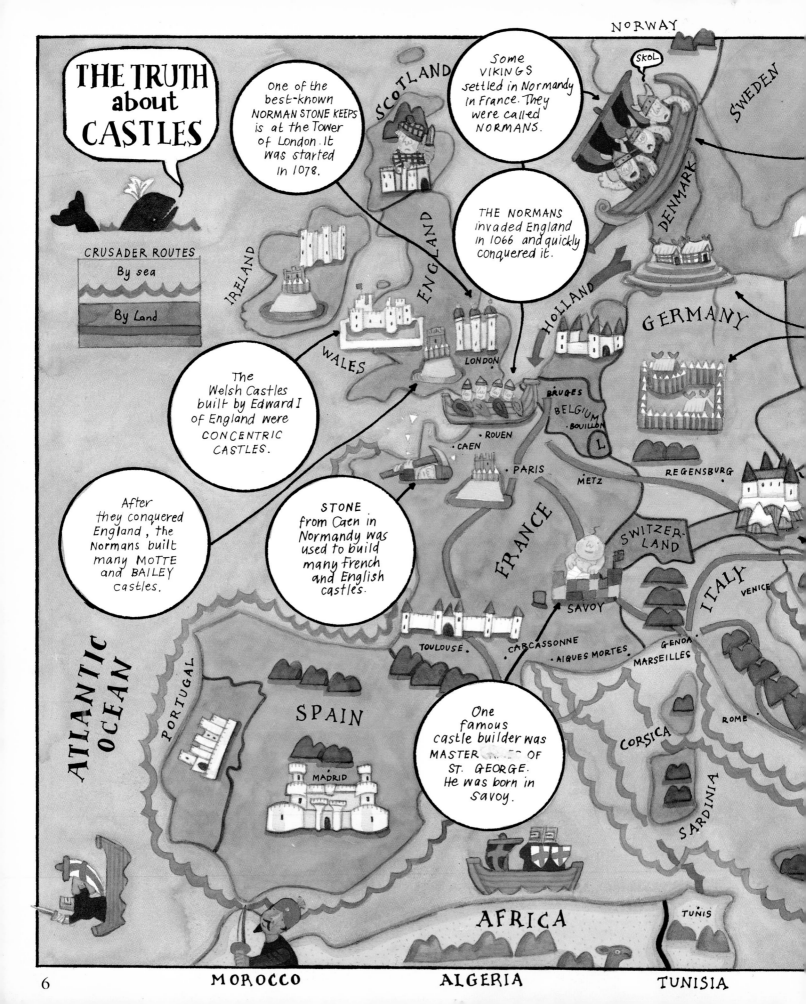

WHAT IS A CASTLE?

A castle is the fortified house of a lord and his followers, from which the lord can rule his lands and be safe from attack.

MOTTE AND BAILEY CASTLES consist of a high mound (or motte) of earth on which a wooden tower overlooks the courtyard (or bailey). Each is protected by a fence and a moat.

STONE KEEPS are very strong three- or four-story castles. They are usually square, with square towers at each corner and a well-defended entrance at the first-floor level.

CONCENTRIC CASTLES have two rings of walls to protect the buildings within. The inner wall and its towers overlook the outer wall so that the attackers can be fired on from any point.

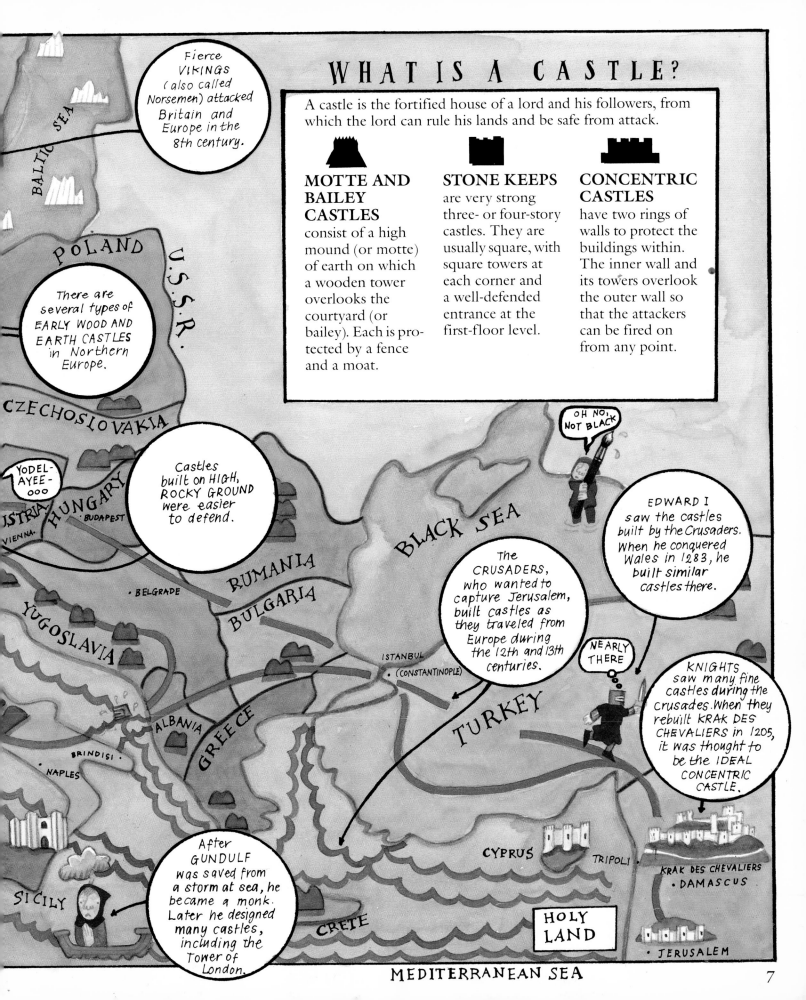

Fierce VIKINGS (also called Norsemen) attacked Britain and Europe in the 8th century.

There are several types of EARLY WOOD AND EARTH CASTLES in Northern Europe.

Castles built on HIGH, ROCKY GROUND were easier to defend.

YODEL-AYEE-OOO

The CRUSADERS, who wanted to capture Jerusalem, built castles as they traveled from Europe during the 12th and 13th centuries.

OH NO, NOT BLACK

EDWARD I saw the castles built by the Crusaders. When he conquered Wales in 1283, he built similar castles there.

NEARLY THERE

KNIGHTS saw many fine castles during the Crusades. When they rebuilt KRAK DES CHEVALIERS in 1205, it was thought to be the IDEAL CONCENTRIC CASTLE.

After GUNDULF was saved from a storm at sea, he became a monk. Later he designed many castles, including the Tower of London.

BALTIC SEA

POLAND

U.S.S.R.

CZECHOSLOVAKIA

AUSTRIA

VIENNA

HUNGARY

BUDAPEST

BELGRADE

YUGOSLAVIA

RUMANIA

BULGARIA

ALBANIA

GREECE

BRINDISI

NAPLES

SICILY

CRETE

BLACK SEA

ISTANBUL (CONSTANTINOPLE)

TURKEY

CYPRUS

TRIPOLI

KRAK DES CHEVALIERS

DAMASCUS

HOLY LAND

JERUSALEM

MEDITERRANEAN SEA

7

A Motte and Bailey Castle

Although many wood and earth castles were built in Europe before 950, it was in that year the Normans built the first motte and bailey castle. When the Normans invaded England in 1066, they needed to build castles quickly in order to protect themselves from the

CASTLES

English. Between 1066 and 1086, the Normans built nearly one hundred motte and bailey castles. These proved to be very effective until stronger castles could be built.

A Stone Keep

THROB

Craftsmen from all over the country, and even abroad, were hired by a constable and then brought to the castle site.

There were many specialist stoneworkers: quarrymen, stone-cutters, and masons.

MUST FEED THE HAMSTER

Treadmills were used for lifting heavy materials.

Besides stoneworkers, craftsmen like mortar-makers, blacksmiths, carpenters, and diggers were needed.

THE TOWER OF LONDON

IT'LL NEVER CATCH ON

In his hut, the master mason drew his plan for the building. At this stage, he rarely used exact measurements.

CONVERSION TABLES
Span, cubit, inch, yard, heaped teaspoonful....

PROPERTY OF MASTER PERRY (MASON)

MASTER MASON H.Q.

Preserved History

Because the buildings and fences were made of wood, motte and bailey castles could be burned down by attackers. The stone keep, however, was much stronger. Its thick stone walls resisted both fire and battering rams. The walls were so thick (up to 13 feet) that

small rooms and staircases were often built inside them. The large rooms of the interior included a great hall and private rooms for the lord and his family.

A Concentric Castle

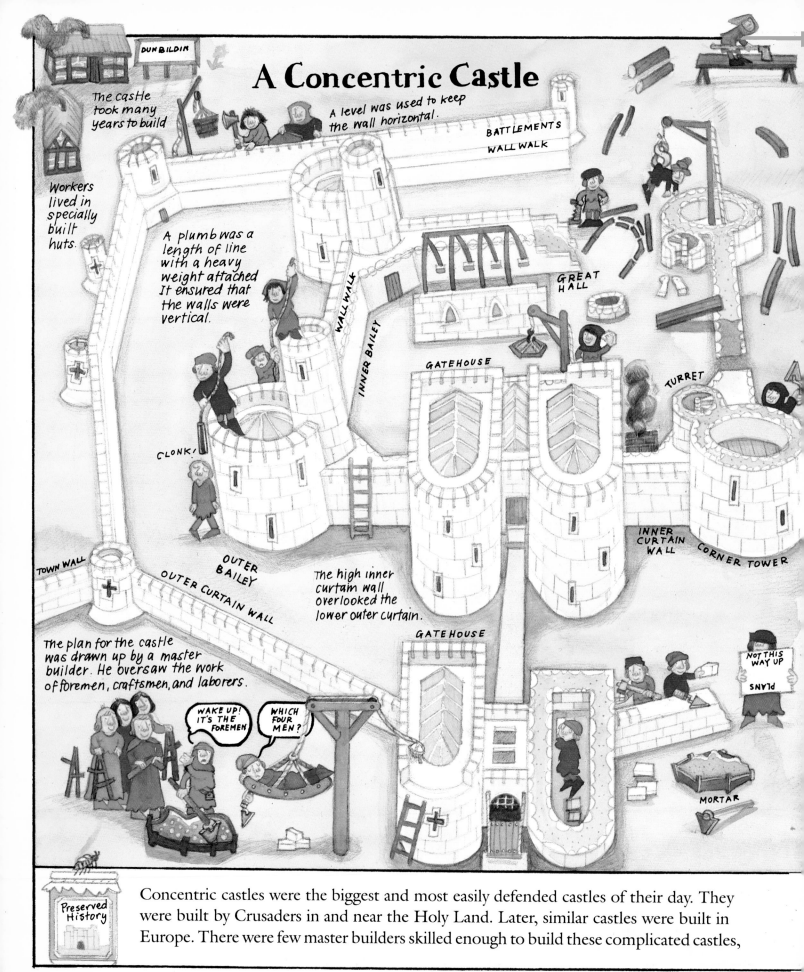

DUN BILDIN

The castle took many years to build

A level was used to keep the wall horizontal.

BATTLEMENTS
WALL WALK

Workers lived in specially built huts.

A plumb was a length of line with a heavy weight attached It ensured that the walls were vertical.

WALL WALK

INNER BAILEY

GREAT HALL

GATEHOUSE

CLONK!

TURRET

OUTER BAILEY

INNER CURTAIN WALL

CORNER TOWER

TOWN WALL

OUTER CURTAIN WALL

The high inner curtain wall overlooked the lower outer curtain.

GATEHOUSE

The plan for the castle was drawn up by a master builder. He oversaw the work of foremen, craftsmen, and laborers.

WAKE UP! IT'S THE FOREMEN

WHICH FOUR MEN?

NOT THIS WAY UP

PLANS

MORTAR

Preserved History

Concentric castles were the biggest and most easily defended castles of their day. They were built by Crusaders in and near the Holy Land. Later, similar castles were built in Europe. There were few master builders skilled enough to build these complicated castles,

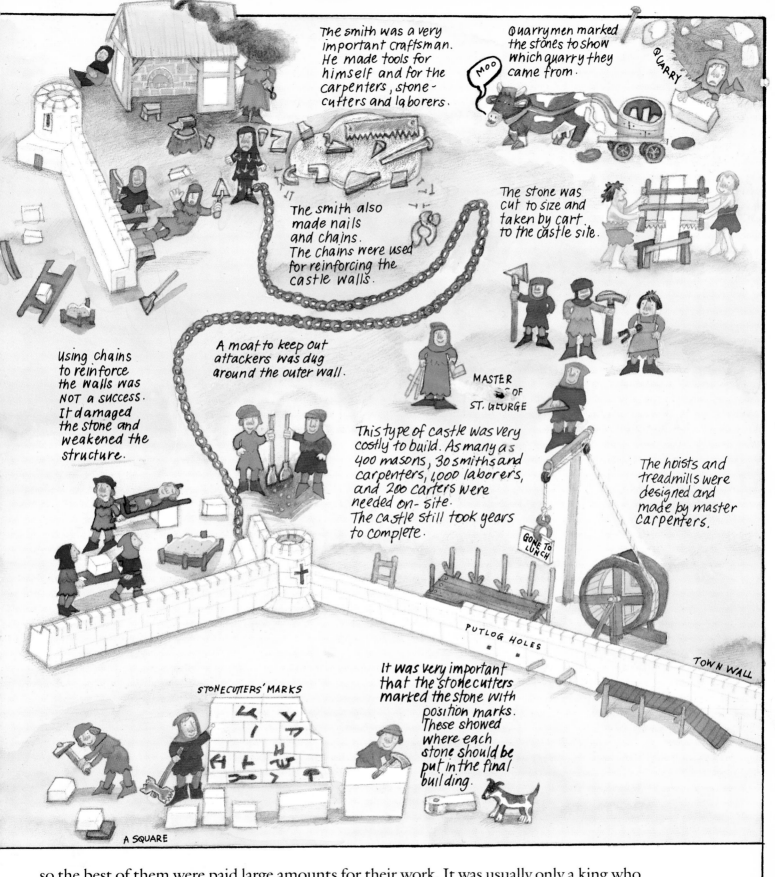

The smith was a very important craftsman. He made tools for himself and for the carpenters, stone-cutters and laborers.

Quarrymen marked the stones to show which quarry they came from.

MOO

QUARRY

The smith also made nails and chains. The chains were used for reinforcing the castle walls.

The stone was cut to size and taken by cart to the castle site.

Using chains to reinforce the walls was NOT a success. It damaged the stone and weakened the structure.

A moat to keep out attackers was dug around the outer wall.

MASTER OF ST. GEORGE

This type of castle was very costly to build. As many as 400 masons, 30 smiths and carpenters, 1,000 laborers, and 200 carters were needed on-site. The castle still took years to complete.

The hoists and treadmills were designed and made by master carpenters.

GONE TO LUNCH

PUTLOG HOLES

TOWN WALL

STONECUTTERS' MARKS

It was very important that the stonecutters marked the stone with position marks. These showed where each stone should be put in the final building.

A SQUARE

so the best of them were paid large amounts for their work. It was usually only a king who could afford the expense. It took hundreds of workers and many years of building to complete even one castle.

THE CASTLE

The Motte and Tower

The Keep

The keep was so strong that it was rarely taken by direct attack. A long siege and the undermining of foundations were more successful.

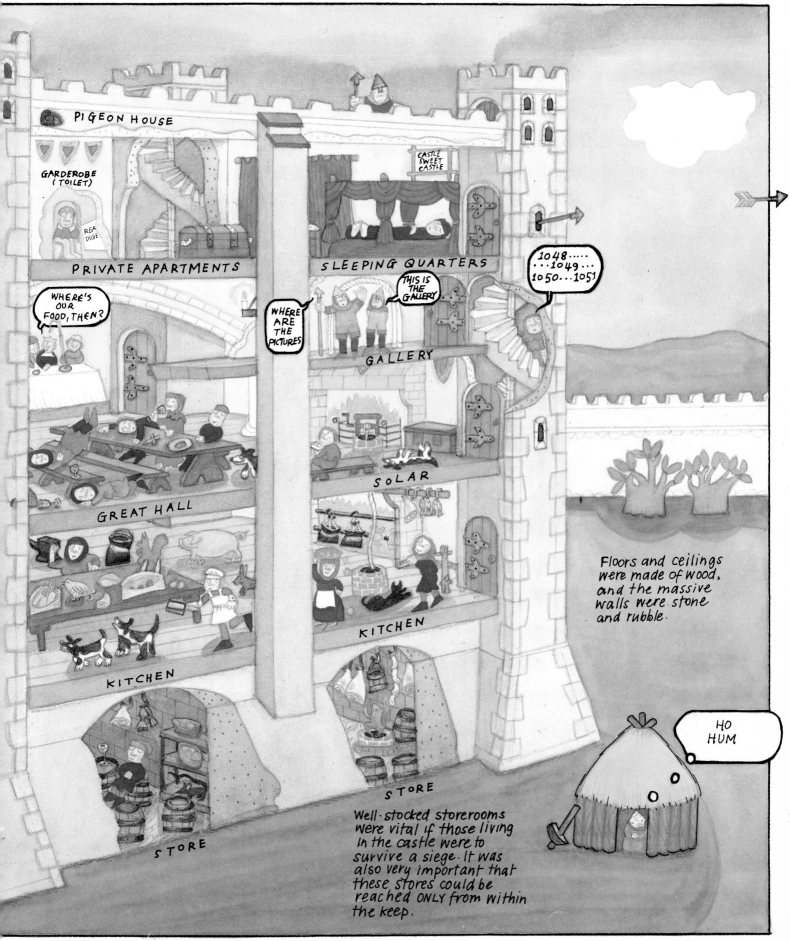

Preparing a Feast

Falcons were kept to hunt hares and rabbits.

Hunting dogs were specially bred in the castle kennels.

Hunting supplied the keep with much of its meat, besides being a favorite pastime for the lord and his friends.

Pages were responsible for taking food from the kitchen to the table.

The Concentric Castle

TOWERS AND WALLS

Walls and towers were vital for the defense of the castle. Soldiers could look out over the outer walls and see the country beyond, so no one could approach the castle unseen.

GASP!! AIR!!

QUICK! OXYGEN!

The interior of the chapel tower was whitewashed.

WALL WALK

Behind the battlements, the wall walk extended around the castle.

Hunting birds were looked after in the castle mews.

?

WE ARE NOT A MEWS

Hunting dogs were very highly prized. Each castle was expected to keep a large pack in its kennels.

KERUNCH!

DID YOU HEAR THE ONE ABOUT.. ....

THE GREAT HALL

APARTMENTS

Feasts were held in the great hall. Lords and ladies sat on a raised platform, and all the diners were entertained by a minstrel, a juggler, or a jester.

THE INNER COURTYARD

DOVECOTE

Apartments were built as private quarters for the lord and lady. There was also a small enclosed garden.

Every boy and man in the castle had to learn archery.

SERVANTS were packed into the ground floor of the apartments.

PEOPLE IN THE CASTLE

Damp cowhide was draped over the wooden palisade to prevent fire.

The massive wooden doors of the gatehouse were barred from the inside.

Vigilant lookouts could spot the enemy a long way off.

Wall towers gave defenders an excellent view and a clear firing line at attackers.

WELL WELL WELL

Fresh water was vital in order to survive a siege.

Like machicolations, hoardings provided protection for the defenders as they fired or dropped stones on to soldiers below.

THIS IS NO PLACE FOR A HORSE

The moat was a useful barrier, making an attack on the castle more dangerous and difficult.

Machicolations were built on to the top of battlements. When a defender walked beneath them, he had water or rocks dropped on his head.

CASTLES

Round towers had an advantage over square towers. When they were bombarded, missiles simply bounced off.

BOING!

Stone replaced wood in some motte and bailey castles.

The view from high walls gave early warning of an attack.

WHAT A LOVELY VIEW

Stairs were designed to hamper attacking swordsmen.

CALL OFF THE ATTACK. I'VE SKINNED MY KNUCKLES

The larger the stock of food, the longer a siege could be withstood.

Thick walls withstood bombardment and direct attack.

TSK

THINK I'LL START MY DIET NOW

Shutters protected archers on the battlements.

Loopholes and gunports came in various shapes and sizes.

Each depended on whether longbows, crossbows, or cannons were used.

BULL'S EYE!

Prince Henry of Scotland was once hooked on a grapnel and almost pulled onto the battlements of the castle he was besieging.

I'VE NEVER SPOKEN TO ONE SO ELEVATED, YOUR HIGHNESS

The barbican was an extra gatehouse. To enter a castle, an enemy had to get past a drawbridge, portcullis, and barred wooden door; pass under "murder holes" at the risk of being struck on the head by a stone; and get through another door. Then he would STILL be outside the moat.

CASTLES

31

IN DECLINE

BUT SOME ARE STILL LIVED IN!

WINDSOR CASTLE

TEN FAMOUS EUROPEAN CASTLES

Baños de la Encina
Jaén, Spain

When the Moors conquered much of Spain in the early 700s, they built Europe's first castles. Baños de la Encina, built in about 967, is one of the most famous of the Moorish castles.

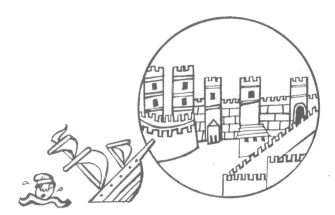

Castel del Monte
central Apulia, Italy

Castel del Monte is an octagonal castle with eight octagonal towers. It was designed by Emperor Frederick II, who ruled the Holy Roman Empire from 1212 to 1250 and was known for his unique castles.

Blarney Castle
Cork, Ireland

Blarney Castle, which was built in about 1446, is the location of the famous Blarney Stone. According to legend, anyone who kisses the Blarney Stone, a large piece of limestone near the battlements of the castle, will be able to speak cleverly and convincingly from that time on.

Castle of Chillon
Montreux, Switzerland

Lord Byron's famous poem "The Prisoner of Chillon" is about a man who revolted against the Duke of Savoy during the 16th century and was imprisoned in the Castle of Chillon for six years. The castle, which stands on a rock in Lake Geneva, was started in the 9th century, but most of it was built in the 13th century.

Chateau Gaillard
Les Andelys, France

Chateau Gaillard was built by Richard I, who is also known as Richard the Lion-Hearted, in Normandy in the 1190s. Richard I was both the king of England and the Duke of Normandy. The castle was meant to defend Normandy, which was not yet part of France, from a French invasion. But the French took the castle in 1204 after a successful siege.

OH NO! THERE'S A GALE BLOWING UP

Gravensteen
Ghent, Belgium
Gravensteen, which is often called the Castle of the Counts, was built by the first Count of Flanders in the ninth century. It is located on a small island in the city of Ghent. Over the years, the castle has undergone many changes and additions.

The Marksburg
Braubach, West Germany
The Marksburg is one of the many castles that were built on the rugged banks of the Rhine River during the Middle Ages. This fortress was the only one of the castles that wasn't captured during the Thirty Years' War in Europe in the early 17th century.

Harlech Castle
Marioneth, Wales
Harlech Castle is one of the famous Welsh castles built by Edward I and his architect, Master James of St. George, during the late 13th and early 14th centuries. The castles were based on those that Edward saw in the Holy Land during the Crusades. Harlech Castle, which was begun in about 1285, is known for the many sieges it underwent.

Windsor Castle
Windsor, England
Windsor Castle is one of the homes of the rulers of Great Britain. The original structure was built by the Norman king William I after he conquered England in 1066. Edward III had this building torn down in the 14th century and replaced it with a much more luxurious castle.

Tower of London
London, England
The Tower of London is actually a group of buildings that includes a prison, a fortress, and royal living quarters. It was built for William I, also called William the Conquerer, by Gundulf of Bec in the 1070s. Now this famous castle houses the British crown jewels.

GLOSSARY

Bailey—an open courtyard within the walls of a castle

Ballista—a giant crossbow used to shoot large, heavy objects at a target

Barbican—an extra gatehouse positioned in front of a castle's main gatehouse

Battlements—defensive walls with toothlike projections

Constable—an official who helps the lord govern his household

Farrier—a person who shoes horses

Herald—a messenger

Hoardings—wooden shields attached to battlements

Loophole—a small opening in a wall through which a weapon can be fired

Machicolation—an opening in a projecting castle wall through which objects can be dropped on enemies

Man-at-arms—a heavily armed soldier in the castle's permanent defensive force

Mangonel—a weapon with a spoon-shaped arm that is used to throw objects at a target

Mantlet—a movable wooden shelter used for protection when attacking

Mews—houses for trained hawks

Moat—a deep, wide ditch that surrounds a castle and is usually filled with water

Motte—a mound of earth, usually topped by a tower, located within or next to a bailey

Page—a person being trained for the knighthood who is a servant to a knight

Palisade—a fence made of pointed wooden stakes

Portcullis—an iron grating that can be pulled down over a castle entrance

Serf—a peasant required to serve a lord

Siege—the act of blocking people in a city or castle while attacking from the outside

Solar—the lord and lady's main sitting room

Squire—a person of noble birth who is training for the knighthood

Steward—the person who manages the castle and the people who work there

Trebuchet—a large weapon with an arm ending in a sling that is used to throw objects at a target

INDEX